Stories in ART

# Sculpture

Richard Spilsbury

WAYLAND

First published in Great Britain in 2008 by Hodder & Stoughton

A catalogue record for this book is available from the British Library.

ISBN 978 0 7502 9486 7

Acknowledgments
Senior Editor: Claire Shanahan
Designer: Rachel Hamdi/Holly Fulbrook
Project Maker: Anna-Marie d'Cruz
Models: Rheanne Khokar, Alex Watson
Photographer: Andy Crawford

Title pages, p14/15: AFP/Getty Images; p6: Scott Barbour/Getty Images; p7: Private
Collection/Photo © Heini Schneebeli/The Bridgeman Art Library; p8: ©
tradewinds/Alamy; p9: Museum of Fine Arts, Houston, Texas, USA, Agnes Cullen
Arnold Endowment Fund/The Bridgeman Art Library; p10/11: Matias Planas/Shutterstock;
p12/13: Terracotta Army, Qin Dynasty, 210 BC; warriors (detail) by
Tomb of Qin shi Huang Di, Xianyang, China/The Bridgeman Art Library; p16/17:
Tipus's Tiger, c.1790 (wood) by Indian School, (18th century), Victoria & Albert
Museum, London, UK/The Bridgeman Art Library; p18/19: Raising the flag on Iwo
Jima, US Marine Corps Memorial, Arlington National Cemetery, Washington DC
(photo) by American Photographer (20th century), Private Collection/Peter Newark
Pictures/The Bridgeman Art Library; p20/21: Haida Eagle clan totem pole (painted
wood) by Canadian School, Private Collection/ Photo © Boltin Picture Library/The
Bridgeman Art Library

Printed in China

An imprint of
Hachette Children's Group
Part of Hodder & Stoughton
Carmelite House
50 Victoria Embankment
London EC4Y 0DZ

An Hachette UK Company
www.hachette.co.uk

www.hachettechildrens.co.uk

# Contents

What is sculpture?     6

How are sculptures made?     8

**Artwork case studies**     **10-21**

Ruler of All Egypt     10

The Terracotta Army     12

The Elephant-Headed God     14

Tipu's Tiger     16

Raising the Flag of Victory     18

Strength of an Eagle     20

**Projects**     **22-27**

Make a wire sculpture     22

Sculpt figures     24

Make a totem pole     26

Glossary     28

Find out more     29

Index     30

# What is sculpture?

A sculpture is a **three-dimensional** work of art. Three-dimensional means something that is not flat – it has **height**, width and depth. Some sculptures can be viewed from all sides, while some are in relief – the form is **carved** or **modelled** from a flat background. Sculptures can be life-size, or much bigger or much smaller. Some sculptures are just for looking at or touching, but others are so big you can walk among or through them!

## What are sculptures made from?

There are many different kinds of sculptures and a variety of different materials. Some sculptures are made from hard materials such as wood, metal and stone. Others could be made of anything, even ice, chocolate or sand – so a sandcastle on a beach could be described as a kind of sculpture! Some sculptures are made from found or natural objects. Many sculptures are of people, but sculptures can be of anything, from animals to aircraft. Some sculptures are not realistic. They do not look like anything in particular, but express a feeling or mood instead.

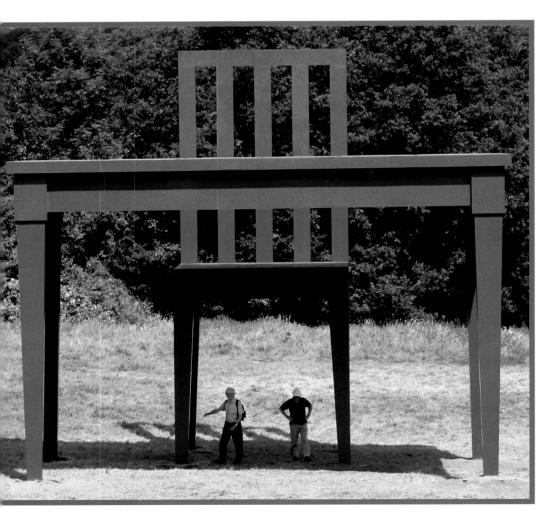

◀ *This is a giant sculpture of a table and chair made from steel and wood by artist Giancarlo Neri. The people underneath are normal height adults!*

# History of sculpture

People have been making sculptures for thousands of years. Before people could write or leave written records of their lives and religious beliefs, sculptures were often used to tell stories or to act as **symbols** to represent something important. Stone Age people made statues and carvings of animals and people out of stone and ivory. On Easter Island, there are more than 600 huge carved stone statues of big heads made around a thousand years ago. No one knows why they were made. Some sculptures are made to protect entrances or make a palace or public building look important, but other sculptures are purely decorative.

▶ *Some ancient sculptures have survived for centuries. This Greek statue of a goddess was carved from stone over 2,200 years ago.*

# How to use this book

Background information on each sculpture featured, including its designer, date, location and history

### Raising the Flag of Victory

This statue is a famous war memorial in Washington, D.C., the capital of the USA. It shows one of the most famous incidents of World War II involving American soldiers called **Marines**. They fought bravely to take over the Pacific Island of Iwo Jima from Japanese soldiers in 1945. This was an important victory that led to the eventual defeat of Japan. The memorial is dedicated to all the Marines who died defending the USA.

Each marine is over 10 metres tall. Artist Felix de Weldon carved a lifesize plaster sculpture based on the real Marines. Then workers at a studio cut it into pieces and used them to create a much bigger version cast in bronze. The parts were made into 12 pieces, some of which weighed over 20 tonnes. These pieces were transported in trucks to the cemetery where the memorial was to be built. They were then fixed together with bolts and melted metal.

*The Marine Corps War Memorial Felix de Weldon 1954 23m high Arlington National Cemetery, Washington, D.C., USA*

### The Story Behind the Art

*By February 1945, US troops had recaptured most of the territory taken by the Japanese in 1941 and 1942 during World War II. However, Japanese forces still held Iwo Jima, a small island south of Japan. On the morning of 19 February 1945, Marines were ordered to fight and capture Mount Suribachi, a high mountain that makes up the narrow southern tip of the island. Four hard days later, soldiers fighting on the mountain slopes saw a small American flag flying on Mount Suribachi. The sight encouraged them to fight on and clear all enemies from the slopes. Then five Marines and a naval medical officer raised a second, larger flag and a newspaper reporter took a photo. This became a famous image back in the USA and was later reproduced as the sculpture.*

### Eye Spy

The 20-metre flagpole is bronze with a real cloth US flag on top. The same flag flies day and night in permanent tribute to all US Marines who died defending their country.

The positions of the figures show us that the Marines used all their strength and worked together to raise the US flag on Iwo Jima.

This section tells you about the story behind each sculpture

Take a closer look at the details in each sculpture

# How are sculptures made?

Sculptures are made in a variety of ways.
Here are four main methods.

▲ *This sculptor is hammering a sharp chisel against a stone block to carve the shape of a dog's head.*

## Carving

In carving, the artist cuts away from a block of solid material to create a sculpture. Sculptures are often carved from marble or other stones, or wood. Artists use tools such as hammers or chisels. Some wood carvers carve sculptures from wood using chainsaws. Larger bits are cut off in pieces and then details are added by careful chiselling or scraping. Sometimes artists also carve softer materials, such as soap or ice.

## Modelling

To model a sculpture, the artist takes a softish material such as clay and **moulds** it with their hands or using tools. When the final shape is made, texture can be added by pressing shapes into the model or cutting into it with other tools. This structure is fired (cooked) or allowed to dry, so that it sets hard. Sculptures can be modelled from many materials including plaster, papier-mâché, wax and bent wire. A completed model can be left as it is or finished off with decoration such as paint.

## Casting

Casting means to make a sculpture using a mould. This is rather like the way you make jelly in a mould. **Cast** sculptures are usually made from **bronze**, steel or plastic. In the 'lost wax' method, an object is made of wax and coated in clay. When the clay is fired, the wax melts and is drained away leaving an exact impression of the object in the hardened clay, which is then filled with molten (melted) metal. The metal cools and hardens and the sculpture is finished.

◄ Look at the detail in this warrior's face and costume. The panel or **plaque** was cast from bronze using the lost wax method over 200 years ago in West Africa.

## Constructing

**Constructed** sculptures are made from different materials combined and joined together to form a three-dimensional object. The pieces can be joined in a variety of ways, including gluing, nailing, taping or even tying together. Metal constructions might be welded (melted) together. Constructed sculptures can be made from new materials, or found materials and junk. Some sculptures are made from reclaimed materials such as old CDs and washing machine parts!

# Ruler of All Egypt

The Great Temple of **Pharaoh** (King) Ramesses II was carved from a mountain overlooking the River Nile, Egypt, over 3,000 years ago. Each giant statue is of the pharaoh seated on a throne decorated with gods of the Nile. He built the **temple** for worship but also to show how important he was. The statues show that Ramesses was a mighty and powerful ruler of all Egypt.

▼ *Ramesses II 1225 BCE 20m high x 35m wide Great Temple of Abu Simbel, Egypt*

# The Story Behind the Art

Ramesses was just 15 when he became pharaoh. Although inexperienced in ruling, he faced serious challenges almost immediately. The Hittites, who lived in what is now Turkey, attacked Ramesses' armies to try to take over part of the empire. The young ruler was nearly trapped and captured in a fierce battle before reinforcements arrived to save the day.

Back home, Ramesses claimed a huge victory and started a publicity campaign to convince his people and everyone else of his greatness. He built many monuments to himself and even inscribed his own name on statues of other rulers!

Privately, he knew he couldn't defeat the Hittites so signed a peace treaty with them instead. Then he set out on a building programme greater than anything ever seen, including the two temples at Abu Simbel for himself and his favourite wife, Nefertiti.

By the time Ramesses died at 93 years of age, he had had many wives and over 100 children. Many of his people fell into deep mourning because they had been born during his magnificent reign and they thought the world would end without him.

## Eye Spy

Ramesses wears the double crown of Upper and Lower Egypt. His young, handsome face is finely carved and his smiling lips are over a metre wide.

Ramesses' mother Tuya, his Chief Wife Nefertiti and some of his many children can be seen in smaller scale at his feet. Beneath these giant sculptures are carved figures of bound captives.

The temple is dedicated to the sun god Re-Harakhte. He is shown with the head of a falcon. Carvings of baboons at the top of the temple are shown raising their hands in worship of the sun.

# The Terracotta Army

The Terracotta Army is a set of life-size sculptures buried with a Chinese **emperor** in 210 BCE. The army is made up of over 8,000 clay soldiers, horses, chariots and buildings. These numerous sculptures were made to help Emperor Shihuang rule another empire in the afterlife. It is thought that it took 700,000 workers and craftsmen 38 years to complete the army. The terracotta Army was discovered in 1974 by local farmers digging a water well.

▼ *Terracotta Army*
*210 BCE*
*1.8m – 1.97m high*
*Xi'an, Northern China*

# The Story Behind the Art

Emperor Shihuang united China. He made everyone use the same sort of money and started building the Great Wall of China, which protected the country from armies attacking from the west. However, he was a mean ruler and made many enemies during his life. Shihuang believed after death he would live on in a different world. But gods he had angered by his cruelty on earth could attack him there. So Shihuang had a vast terracotta army made, to be buried alongside him in a massive **tomb** after his death. Each soldier was armed and ready to fight for him in the afterlife. Shihuang was such a cruel emperor that he ordered the sculptors working on the project to be buried alive with him, so that no secrets of the tomb could ever be revealed!

 **Eye Spy**

The soldiers wear outfits ranging from armour and belted tunics to coats of chain mail and wind-proof caps. The soldiers were probably modelled in clay sections and the parts fired separately before being stuck together.

There are slight differences in the complexions, expressions, ages, hairstyles and beards of each warrior. Some people think they may have been modelled on living soldiers. Each was originally painted in bright colours which have now faded to white.

# The Elephant-Headed God

Ganesh is a Hindu god with a human body and an elephant's head and he is important in Hindu religion. **Hinduism** is a religion that began in Asia over 3,000 years ago. Ganesh is known as the protector or Remover of Obstacles. People often pray to him when they are starting a new business or they place him at entrances to protect themselves.

▶ *Ganesh*
*20th century*
*5m high*
*Hyderabad, India*

# The Story Behind the Art

*Lord Shiva, the Hindu god of death and destruction, was away at a war. While he was away, his wife the goddess Pavarti gave birth to a son she named Ganesh. She instructed Ganesh to guard the entrance of her rooms and not to allow anyone in. Lord Shiva returned from war earlier than expected. When he tried to enter Pavarti's rooms, Ganesh stopped him. Shiva did not know Ganesh and was enraged by his impudence. Shiva immediately drew his sword and cut off Ganesh's head.*

*Pavarti came running from her rooms to find Ganesh without his head and she flew into a rage. To make amends, Shiva promised to take the head of the first living thing he found to replace Ganesh's head. The first animal he came across was an elephant, and that is why Ganesh is always shown with an elephant's head.*

 ## Eye Spy

Ganesh usually holds a plate or bowl of sweet food in his hand or sometimes in his trunk. The sweet is a joyful reward because he is successful in seeking truth. Ganesh's belly is fat because of all the sweets and therefore the wisdom it contains!

This Ganesh statue has lots of arms each holding different objects that tell us about his character. The lotus flower is a symbol of truth and beauty.

The symbol painted on Ganesh's hand is *om* or *aum*. In Hindu belief, om is a divine sound. It is the first sound of creation from which life emerged.

# Tipu's Tiger

This is Tipu's Tiger, a carved and painted wooden sculpture. It shows a tiger attacking a British soldier. The sculpture was commissioned by and belonged to Sultan Tipu. Tipu was a king who ruled a large part of southern India with a well-trained army and fair government. He fought against British forces who were trying to rule India.

Tipu was famous for saying, 'Better to live a day as a tiger than a lifetime as a sheep'. In other words, he thought it better to die while being brave and free, rather than to live a long life as a coward, kept by others.

▼ *Tipu's Tiger*
*18th century*
*Life-size*
*Victoria & Albert Museum,*
*London, England, UK*

# The Story Behind the Art

Tipu was sultan of Mysore in south India from 1782 to 1799. At this time, Britain already ruled parts of India and was trying to extend its power there. Mysore was one of the most powerful states in India and fought the British with a vengeance.

Tigers and tiger symbols adorned most of Tipu's possessions, from his magnificent throne to the uniforms of his guards. He even had cannons with tigers on and hand weapons decorated with gold tiger heads. Live tigers were kept in the city and there were stories of prisoners thrown into the tiger-pits. Tipu thought of himself as a mighty, royal tiger, who was appointed by God to devour God's enemies, the British.

Between 1762 and 1799, there were four Mysore wars. In 1799, the state finally fell to the British and Tipu died fighting bravely in the struggle for the capital city. The British seized many of his belongings as trophies, including the wooden tiger. Eventually Britain took control of the whole of India and the country remained under British rule until 1947.

 ## Eye Spy

It is thought that Tipu had this sculpture made around 1790 after hearing a story. A young Englishman out shooting near Calcutta was carried off and killed by an immense tiger. It symbolised Tipu's longed-for defeat of the British, which never came.

When you turn the crank-handle by the tiger's shoulder, it makes a wheezy roaring sound and the soldier's hand moves up and down. The sounds simulate the growls of the tiger and the cries of its victim!

# Raising the Flag of Victory

This statue is a famous war memorial in Washington, D.C., the capital of the USA. It shows one of the most famous incidents of World War II involving American soldiers called **Marines**. They fought bravely to take over the Pacific Island of Iwo Jima from Japanese soldiers in 1945. This was an important victory that led to the eventual defeat of Japan. The memorial is dedicated to all the Marines who died defending the USA.

▶ *The Marine Corps War Memorial*
*Felix de Weldon*
*1954*
*23m high*
*Arlington National Cemetery,*
*Washington, D.C., USA*

Each marine is over 10 metres tall. Artist Felix de Weldon carved a lifesize plaster sculpture based on the real Marines. Then workers at a studio cut it into pieces and used them to create a much bigger version cast in bronze. The parts were made into 12 pieces, some of which weighed over 20 tonnes. These pieces were transported in trucks to the cemetery where the memorial was to be built. They were then fixed together with bolts and melted metal.

UNCOMMON VALOR WAS A COMMON VIRTUE

# The Story Behind the Art

By February 1945, US troops had recaptured most of the territory taken by the Japanese in 1941 and 1942 during World War II. However, Japanese forces still held Iwo Jima, a small island south of Japan. On the morning of 19 February 1945, Marines were ordered to fight and capture Mount Suribachi, a high mountain that makes up the narrow southern tip of the island. Four hard days later, soldiers fighting on the mountain slopes saw a small American flag flying on Mount Suribachi. The sight encouraged them to fight on and clear all enemies from the slopes. Then five Marines and a naval medical officer raised a second, larger flag and a newspaper reporter took a photo. This became a famous image back in the USA and was later reproduced as the sculpture.

## Eye Spy

The 20-metre flagpole is bronze with a real cloth US flag on top. The same flag flies day and night in permanent tribute to all US Marines who died defending their country.

The positions of the figures show us that the Marines used all their strength and worked together to raise the US flag on Iwo Jima.

# Strength of an Eagle

**Totem poles** were carved and erected by **Native Americans** of northwest USA and Canada. They are symbols of their family or **tribe**. Totem poles often told family histories or stories of the different tribes. This is a Haida Eagle totem pole. The Haida people live on islands on the coast of British Columbia. The stories of the poles are told by parents to their children, so they are remembered year after year.

Animals carved on totem poles are used to represent the different characteristics or strengths of a family or tribe. For example, orca whales are travellers, guardians and symbols of good, whereas frogs represent spring and new life.

▶ *Haida Eagle clan totem pole 20th century Private collection*

# The Story Behind the Art

The Haida tribe lived along calm and sheltered beaches by forests. They were the most feared coastal North American Indians. The tribe was divided into two clans (groups): the ravens and eagles. It is said the Haida possessed the Eagle's strength and the raven's cunning in battle.

The tribe used tall cedar tree trunks from the forests for many purposes. For example, they carved and rowed canoes to raid or to trade with nearby tribes. Some canoes were massive – carved from a single cedar tree – and were as long as 15 adults head to toe! The Haida also used the tall cedar tree trunks to make totem poles. They made totems for different reasons, such as to honour the death of a relative.

They carved animals and symbols from bottom to top of the totems. The symbols at the bottom were often more finely carved than those at the top because they were closer to the viewer. Paint to colour the totem poles was made from natural products, such as copper for the green-blue and clamshells to make white. The clans raised their totems using ropes and wooden props. Totem-raising was a special event, and often happened during huge parties called Potlatches. As they raised the pole, the Haida sang and danced and beat drums and shook rattles.

 **Eye Spy**

The eagle or thunderbird at the top of this totem pole is a symbol of the Haida tribe. In Haida legends, thunderbirds ruled the sky and occasionally flew to earth to catch whales to eat. When thunderbirds fought massive battles, there was thunder and lightning.

The wolf is shown biting into a fish. Wolves symbolise intelligence and leadership. In Haida legend, wolves also care for their relatives and can heal sickness.

# Make a wire sculpture

## What you do:

**1** Gently bend a pipe cleaner in half. Twist a big loop to form the shape of the head. Twist again further down and separate the two ends to make legs. Bend ends to make feet.

**2** Bend a second pipe cleaner in half and wrap it around the 'body' of the first pipe cleaner to make arms. Bend over the ends to make hands.

**Top Tip!**
It's fun to take a digital photograph of someone in a pose so that you can copy it when you're making your sculpture!

**3** Bend the body so that it is dancing or even doing a headstand! Standing your figure up may prove difficult unless you give it big feet!

**4** Tape on scrunched up bits of newspaper to fill the head. Wrap strips of newspaper around the body, arms and legs to add padding. Check your figure balances as you go along, as you may need to make adjustments whilst adding the newspaper.

**5** Then cover the whole figure with small bits of newspaper stuck on with PVA glue. This will help make the figure strong and cover any remaining bits of pipe cleaner.

**6** Once this is dry, you can paint the figure.

You can experiment with decorating your wire sculpture in other materials. Why not cover it with silver foil to make it look like silver? Or create a brushed bronzed effect by covering the wire with Modroc, painting it black first and then with bronze-coloured paint. Finally, rub some of the paint off.

23

# Sculpt figures

Here are two ways of making figures.

## Clay people

### What you do:

**1** Take a lump of air-drying clay and start to mould the shape of your figure. Try to make your figure out of one piece of clay and avoid making standing figures, as these may break.

**2** Use tools to model and make marks in the figure.

**Top Tip!**
Think about what positions you like to relax in, such as lying down cross-legged or sitting with your knees raised up. Practising these positions will help you to sculpt a realistic figure.

**3** When your sculpture has dried out, paint it with poster paint.

# Salt dough sculpting

## What you do:

**1** Plan the design for your sculpture on paper. Perhaps you could use an animal design?

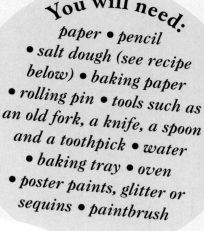

### You will need:
paper • pencil
• salt dough (see recipe below) • baking paper
• rolling pin • tools such as an old fork, a knife, a spoon and a toothpick • water
• baking tray • oven
• poster paints, glitter or sequins • paintbrush

### Recipe for salt dough

*Mix 1 cup of salt and 2 cups of plain flour together in a bowl. Then, slowly add 1 cup of hot water (from the tap) hand kneed the dough until it feels elastic. If the mixture is too sticky, add more flour. If it's too dry, add more water.*

**2** Roll out the salt dough about 1cm deep. Place your template from step 1 on top of the salt dough and cut out the shape with a blunt knife.

**Top Tip!**
Place baking paper beneath the dough so that it is easier to transfer to a baking tray later on.

**3** Add details to your sculpture using the tools and if you want to create a layered effect, stick on pieces of dough using a little water.

**4** Carefully place the sculpture on to a baking tray and ask an adult to put it in the oven on a low temperature for approximately an hour. Test it is fired (cooked) hard all the way through using a toothpick.

**5** When the sculpture has cooled, paint and decorate it.

# Make a totem pole

You could create a totem pole that represents your family history. Think of some animals or symbols that represent your family. Perhaps your mother is like a wise owl and your younger brother is like a puppy dog?

**You will need:**
sugar paper
• paper towel tube
• ruler • coloured pencils, paint or markers • brown paper
• safety scissors
• glue stick

## What you do:

**1** Measure the paper towel tube's height and width with a ruler. Trim a piece of paper to the same size, allowing a 1cm overlap around the tube to glue the edges together.

**2** On the sugar paper, draw and colour in three or four different animal heads in the centre, one above the other. These will go at the front of the totem pole.

**3** Wrap and glue the paper around the tube. Make sure you glue the seam firmly at the back.

**4** Draw pairs of wings or arms for each of the animals on another piece of paper. Decorate them and cut them out.

**5** Glue them to the back of the totem pole.

## Class totem

*If your class wants to make a totem pole, you could work in groups to model several more clay animal faces, paint and fire them in a kiln (oven). Then these could be attached one above the other on a tall piece of wood to make a totem pole that can brighten up a dull corner of your school playground!*

# Glossary

**bronze**   metal made of mixture of copper and tin that does not rust and is good for making sculptures

**carve**   cut by removing the surface of a piece of material

**cast**   make shape such as a sculpture using a shaped mould

**construct**   put together using different parts

**emperor**   powerful ruler of a country, its government and its army

**Hinduism**   major religion in India and other parts of the world. Hindus believe in many gods and think that their soul is reborn in a new body after death

**Marine**   a type of US soldier who serves both on land and at sea

**model**   to form using clay or other soft material

**mould**   hollow shape used to produce a sculpture

**Native American**   person with ancestors who were the original inhabitants of North America before European settlers arrived

**pharoah**   ancient Egyptian king

**plaque**   flat panel sculpture where modelled shapes stick out from the background

**symbol**   object, figure or character that represents something else, such as an idea or belief

**temple**   place of worship

**three-dimensional**   something with height,  width and depth

**tomb**   grave or monument to dead people

**totem pole**   large, wooden sculpture with symbols of certain Native American tribes

**tribe**   group of people related by birth and sharing the same language and culture

# Find out more

## Books to read

*Clay Modelling* (Step-by-Step Children's Craft) by Greta Speechley (Search Press, 2000)

*Sculpture* (Directions in Art) by Jillian Powell (Heinemann, 2004)

*Sculpture* (Let's Start Art) by Sue Nicholson (RIC, 2007)

*Sculpture: Three Dimensions in Art* (Artventure) by Anne Civardi (Wayland, 2005)

*Wood Artists and Stone Artists* (Artists at Work) by Cheryl Jakab (Macmillan Education, 2006)

## Websites to visit

Take a virtual tour through a sculpture garden at www.nga.gov/kids/kids.htm.

Make a sculpture from junk at www.tate.org.uk/learning/kids/zoomroom/junkysculpture.htm.

Explore sculptures by artist, type of material used and when made at www.artcyclopedia.com/media/Sculptor.html.

Does sculpture have a purpose? What do sculptors create with? These are just some of the questions answered at www.childrensmuseum.org/artsworkshop/sculpture/index.html.

## Places to go

Sculpture parks are fantastic places to enjoy art without being inside a gallery.
Try one of the following:
Yorkshire Sculpture Park, West Bretton, Wakefield, Yorkshire
Grizedale Forest, Cumbria

Museums and art galleries have loads of examples of sculptures. Here are just a few.
For ancient sculptures: The British Museum, London, or National Gallery of Scotland, Edinburgh
For sculptures from places all around the world: Pitt Rivers Museum, Oxford
For modern sculptures made of many different materials: Tate Britain or Tate Modern, London; Tate St Ives, St Ives, Cornwall; Tate, Liverpool

Some sculpture is easy to see when out and about. Look out for:
The Angel of the North, near the A1 road, Gateshead, Tyne and Wear
Willow Man, near the M5 motorway, Bridgewater, Somerset
Nelson's Column and four statues of lions, in Trafalgar Square, London

# Index

Photos or pictures are shown below in bold, **like this**.

artists  8, 18

bronze  9, **9**, 18-19, **18-19**

carvings  6, 7, 8, **8**, 10-11, **10**, 16-17,
  **16-17**, 20
casting  9, **9**
clay  8, 9, 12-13, **12-13**, 24, **24**, 27

de Weldon, Felix  18

Easter Island  7

firing  8, 9, 27

marble  8
materials 6, 8, 9 *also* see specific types
  e.g. wood
metals  6, **6**, 9, 18
models and modelling  6, 8, 13, **13**,
  22-3, **22-3**
moulds  9

Native Americans  20-21

papier-mâché  8
plaster  8, 18

sculptors  **8**, 13
sculptures  6-9, **6-9**
  ancient 7, **7**, 10-13, **10-13**
  constructed  9
  Hindu  14-15, **14-15**

statues  7, **7**, 10-11, **10**, 18-19, **18-19**
stone  6, 7, **7**, 8, **8**
symbols  7, 20-21, **20-21**, 26

Terracotta Army  12-13, **12-13**
textures  8
Tipu's Tiger  16-17, **16-17**
tools  8, **8**
totem poles  20-21, **20-21**, 26-7, **26-7**

wax  8, 9
wire  8, 22-3, **22-3**
wood  6, **6**, 8, 16-17, **16-17**